Risk Management Fundamentals

An introduction to risk management in the financial services industry in the 21st century

Written by Justin C McCarthy

I0106539

PRMIA
Professional Risk Managers' International Association

Professional Risk Managers' International Association (PRMIA)

Copyright © 2023 Professional Risk Managers' International Association (PRMIA)

All Rights Reserved.

No part of this publication may be reproduced, distributed, or transmitted in any form or by any means, including photocopying, recording, or other electronic or mechanical methods, without the prior written permission of the publisher, except in the case of brief quotations, embodied in critical reviews and certain other noncommercial uses permitted by copyright law.

For permissions requests, write to the publisher, addressed "Attention: Permissions Coordinator" at the address below.

Cover Design by: Ragib Shahriar

ISBN (Digital online): 979-8-9861646-9-4
ISBN (eBook): 979-8-9876549-0-3
ISBN (Paperback): 979-8-9876549-1-0

PRMIA
1700 Cannon Rd, Suite 200, Northfield, MN 55057
Support@PRMIA.org

www.PRMIA.org

Why Learn About Risk Management?

Although financial risk management as a profession did not exist just a few decades ago, understanding risk has been at the heart of financial services for some time in the following ways:

- In banking, know whether to give a loan and how much interest should be charged
- In insurance, knowing the probability and impact of an insured event
- In funds and the markets, deciding on which shares to invest on to make a profit and avoid a loss

In recent years, the role of risk manager and the place of the risk management function has grown. By the turn of the new millennium many firms had credit, market, and operational risk functions in place. It was the great financial crisis of the late 2000s that accelerated this trend.

Whether driven by an understanding that a more holistic view of risk management was required or through the urging of financial regulators and others, there was an increase in the types and amounts of risk categories being managed and many firms wanted a Chief Risk Officer to join their senior management.

This book starts with the basics of risk management and works through to risk categories that are getting more attention, such as strategic and business model risk.

This book introduces risk and risk management and is intended to provide the basics on risk management. The goal is to present the fundamentals of risk management to promote interest in the topic for further professional development.

Across financial services, risk management is an increasingly valued competency. This book and its related programs serve as an introduction for interested financial services participants including internal auditors, loan officers and those new to the industry.

Learning Outcomes

On successful completion of this book, you should be able to:

- Explain risk and risk management
- Explain the different steps in the risk management process
- Describe market risk and its tools such as value at risk and stress testing
- Describe credit risk and its participants including credit rating agencies
- Describe liquidity risk and asset liability management, and recent developments
- Describe operational risk and related activities such as investigating operational risk events
- Describe strategic and business model risk and its related tools such as the business model canvas
- Reflect on how risk management may be applied in your own organization

Risk Management and PRMIA

The Professional Risk Managers' International Association (PRMIA) is a non-profit professional association, governed by a Board of Directors directly elected by its global membership. PRMIA is represented globally by dozens of chapters in major cities around the world.

To accomplish its vision for a world in which risk management is a recognized profession and embedded core competency of the financial services industry, PRMIA members and risk leaders work to promote, develop, and share professional risk management practices globally.

PRMIA is active in nearly every major financial center worldwide and provides an extensive and engaged network of risk professionals.

PRMIA
Professional Risk Managers'
International Association

| 40% EUROPE/AFRICA MIDDLE EAST 22 CHAPTERS | 30% AMERICAS 17 CHAPTERS | 30% ASIA/PACIFIC 7 CHAPTERS |

PRMIA offers over 200 meetings each year through local chapters, giving members access to the best practices of the global risk profession and to a local network of colleagues. Executive staff and board members take advantage of the Risk Leader Program, which connects a global network of Chief Risk Officers and the most senior risk professionals.

This book serves as an introduction to risk and risk management and as a first step on a path into the PRMIA certificate programs.

PRMIA offers assessment-based certificate programs on risk categories such as operational risk, credit risk, market risk, and others. A reader with a goal to become a Risk Manager or Risk Analyst may pursue the Professional Risk Manager (PRM™) Designation, a globally recognized, graduate-level leading risk manager credential.

Learn more at www.prmia.org/prm

Chapter 1: Risk and Risk Management

1.1 Introduction

An initial concept to understand is that risk is not a bad thing – some element of risk taking is required to gain rewards, both in finance and in life.

It is the management of this risk that is key. Understanding the probability and impact of risks is the first step in managing risk. Working through the risk process and getting to the point where a risk is being properly mitigated is part of the journey in becoming a risk manager.

This chapter provides an understanding of risk throughout the financial services industry and an understanding that its management is a topic outside of financial services.

1.2 Risk and Risk Management

Before learning about risk management, it is best to understand the concept of risk. Once a person understands that not all risk is dangerous, then a more thoughtful approach to risk management and its mitigation can be considered.

Risk

Risk combines the uncertainty of some event occurring and the additional uncertainty of the effect of that event.

Most importantly, we need to understand that risk may have positive or negative outcomes.

For some, the focus of risk in financial services has been on the negative:

- Excessive risk was taken by banks in concentrating their loans on sub-prime loans. The outcome was huge losses for these banks and knock-on effects to the global economy and society during the Great Recession of the late 2000s.
- Continental Illinois was once one of the largest commercial banks in the United States with approximately $40 billion in assets. During the 1980s it was bailed out due to a liquidity crisis prompted by a flight of wholesale investors and creditors alarmed by the bank's excessive exposure to energy and less developed countries.
- Nick Leeson, an employee in Barings Bank, was able to circumvent internal controls and took on unauthorized market positions. The outcome was losses greater than Barings Bank could absorb resulting in the collapse of the bank.
- Royal Bank of Scotland was involved in the largest bank acquisition ever through a deal to purchase ABN Amro bank. The outcome was a bank overstretched for capital when other parts of its business were stressed by a financial crisis. While the bank survived, its CEO was forced to resign and a multi-billion pound bailout had to be provided by the UK government.

Risk can also be a positive force and result in a reward in financial services. Some examples:

- Extending credit to a customer is rewarded with a series of payments that cover the original loan and reward the credit institution with interest for the use of the funds extended.
- Investing in a bond from an EU Government is rewarded with interest payments for providing funds to allow government services to be financed.
- A firm decides to go into business in a new area – for example selling insurance to car owners as well as providing loans for their cars.

All three scenarios may have adverse outcomes – the loan may end up unpaid, the bond may default, and the insurance business may not make a profit due to premiums not covering claims – but these risks are taken in an attempt to improve a business.

The challenge is to manage this risk to ensure reasonable risks are taken to source rewards without risking too much. This is the relationship between risk and reward. At its simplest, to increase the reward expected, an increase in risk should be expected. The risk and reward relationship is best known in activities such as betting – the more likely a team is to win in a sport, the smaller the expected pay-out is.

To examine risk and reward further, we will return to our example scenarios above:

- Extending credit to a customer

A typical customer may be charged something like 5% interest on their loan. It would be prudent to not accept a member with a history of defaulting on payments on previous loans. However, a decision may be made to charge 10% interest on loans to such customers to cover the potential cost of defaulting loans. This will result in a larger reward if the loans perform due to the larger interest payments. However, this could result in a large loss if many of these loans stopped being paid.

- Investing in a bond from a European Government

A bond from a country like Germany may pay 2% on the bond. A larger amount such as 4% may be paid on the bond of a country that is seen to be more likely to encounter difficulties in repaying the bond. An investor would be well rewarded if they select the 4% bond, but there may be a loss if that bond should default.

- A firm deciding to go into a new business area

A firm may be prudent if they expand into a new area – for example opening new branches at a rate that doubles their sites over several years. However, a boom in the economy may encourage them to double their sites each year to keep up with new demand. The outcome could be less beneficial if there is a sudden change in the economic climate or if the finances of the firm cannot keep up with the expansion of the business.

It is this balance between risk and reward that is at the heart of risk management. Understanding that some risks must be taken to reward a firm while not risking large losses is something all sensible firms must put processes and systems in place to manage.

Risk Management

Risk management is a process which aims to define and understand risks, evaluate the impact and probability of these risks, and take action to mitigate the risks by decreasing the probability of a bad outcome and reducing the related impact of failure.

Figure 1: The Risk Management Process

Identification: There should be a firm-wide review of risk – at a minimum all types of risk as listed throughout this book should be considered.

Assessment and Measurement: The likelihood of a risk occurring and the potential impact of the risk on the firm should be reviewed. There should be an understanding of the difference between inherent risk and residual risk:

- Inherent risk is the risk to the firm with no other mitigation measures. It is usually the risk that is in processes and the business before any internal controls have been put in place.

- Residual risk is the risk to the firm after some element of risk mitigation has been applied. By measuring the effectiveness of internal controls or mitigating actions to the original inherent risk, a measure of the effectiveness of the risk management program can be determined.

Once the residual risk is determined, then risk can be ranked by those most likely to cause a major impact to the firm. This can be done in the risk register and risks can be listed by the different risk types (e.g., credit, liquidity, etc.)

Management: The risks in the firm should be managed through a "risk management system", which should not be confused with commercial risk software packages. The risk management system should be made up of the risk management policy, risk Register, and systems and controls, all with a regular review by management or the board of directors. In addition, the firm must decide how they will manage their risks.

Accepted mitigation techniques are:

- Avoidance (e.g., a firm might withdraw from a certain business area)
- Reduction (e.g., a firm may mitigate risk through a series of internal controls or back-up systems)
- Sharing (e.g., a firm may transfer risk to another party through insurance)
- Retention (e.g., a firm may accept a certain amount of bad loans and budget for them)

Monitoring: The risk management process is not a one-off process; it has to be continuously monitored (e.g., the identification of new and emerging risks if there is a new product, business line or services). Items likes risk mitigation letters from a financial regulator or internal audit reports can be used to refresh the risk register.

Reporting: The risk management function should provide regular reports to management and the board of directors covering items such as any risk events that have occurred and the actions used to mitigate the risks identified, updates on risk management actions arising from previous risk reporting, or significant risks and the effectiveness of systems and controls.

As figure 1 shows, this is a continuous and ongoing process. Each stage must be done on a regular basis to ensure the critical risks to the firm are identified, managed, and reported.

1.3 Risk in Financial Services

Before looking at the risk management system, risk in different parts of the financial services industry can be considered.

Risk in Banking

Traditionally, risk management in banking has been related to credit risk. Banks make loans to their customers and earn an income on the interest paid on these loans. However, if that customer should default on their loan repayments, then the bank will make a loss.

Risk mitigation in banks has included understanding a customer before a loan is made, managing any issues with repayment, and putting aside provisions for any loans which may be at an increased danger of default.

Risk in Insurance

The business of insurance is one in which the insurer undertakes to provide a guarantee of compensation for a specified event such as damage to an asset, illness, or death, in return for payment of a specified premium. However, if the premium does not cover the compensation to customers, then the insurance firm may make a loss.

Risk mitigation in insurance has included applying mathematical and statistical methods to assess risk. However, as premiums are invested in assets to allow additional income, market risk has become a part of this industry. Market risk includes the possibility of a loss or profit from a movement in the financial markets.

Risks in Funds

Investors have long invested in funds to secure a return on their investments. In turn, the fund manager provides this return without losing the funds being invested.

Risk management in funds has traditionally been around market risk but with an increasingly complex ecosystem, operational risk is now becoming a desired skill.

Risk Management is a valued skill outside of the financial services industry.

The same process of identifying, assessing, mitigating, and reporting on risks can be applied in many industries.

In the energy sector, events such as the Deepwater Horizon oil spill have shown where risk management was not properly applied. In addition, as prices for oil and gas fluctuate, companies can have difficulty determining if their selling prices will cover exploration and other costs.

In the aviation sector, there has been a long tradition of investigating and learning the lessons from air disasters and again the fluctuation of fuel prices can have an impact on the profits of an airline.

Finally, strategic and business model risk can be applied to any enterprise. A firm may fail because it is not able to compete at the same prices and product as their competitors. Business model risk can cover this loss if a firm has a viable business model (i.e., the Blockbusters movie rentak chain could not compete with a "Bricks and Mortar" distribution model once firms like Netflix brought an internet-based distribution model)

Figure 2: Risk Management

1.4 The Risk Management System

The risk process may be supported by a risk management system. This system can be made up of systems and controls, the risk register, risk management policy, and appropriate overview by management or the board of directors.

Systems and Controls

Returning to inherent risk (the risk to the firm with no other mitigation measures) and residual risk (the risk to the firm after some element of risk mitigation has been applied), we can introduce the concepts of systems and controls.

Mitigating risk can be achieved by establishing and maintaining effective systems and controls. A simple example may be the physical security of an office building. The inherent risk of a burglary may be quite high but systems and controls like locks on the doors and property insurance can mitigate the risk. The residual risk, like a burglar entering a building by other means, can then be considered and if it is deemed to be acceptable, then the risk can be seen to be sufficiently mitigated.

However, if the building has some particularly critical assets contained within, then additional controls and systems may be required to sufficiently mitigate the risks. It might be decided that security guards and security checks will further mitigate the risk and thus the residual risk is further mitigated.

It is important that the systems and controls match the scale and complexity of the organization and related risks. For example, armed guards, controlled access to missile silos, and highly secured codes may be appropriate for nuclear weapons but are impractical for protecting the stationary supplies in an office.

Matching systems and controls to risks is part of the risk management system and helps to mitigate risks to an appropriate level.

Risk Register

The purpose of the risk register is to facilitate the ownership and management of each risk. It should include the significant risks facing a firm. It will record the results of the risk assessment and the results of mitigating actions.

The risk register records:

- The risks that have been identified and the systems and controls currently undertaken in order to mitigate the level of the risks to an acceptable level
- Any additional actions that are proposed to improve the control of the risk
- Information about the responsibilities for individual risks and the corresponding controls. A deadline for the implementation and the responsibility for implementation of each control can also be added.

It is important that the risk register is regularly reviewed. Management or the board of directors should review the risk register on a regular basis, monthly or quarterly, and more frequently in times of change or during a crisis event. The proper association of probability and impact with each risk allows proper review and mitigating of risks in an efficient manner.

At a minimum, the following should be included in a risk register:

- Risk description
- Inherent impact of risk
- Inherent probability of risk
- Inherent risk rating
- Risk mitigating systems and controls
- Systems and controls owners
- Effectiveness of systems and controls
- Residual impact of risk
- Residual probability of risk
- Residual risk rating

These can be compiled in a number of formats, ranging from a simple spreadsheet document to a sophisticated application with an underlying database.

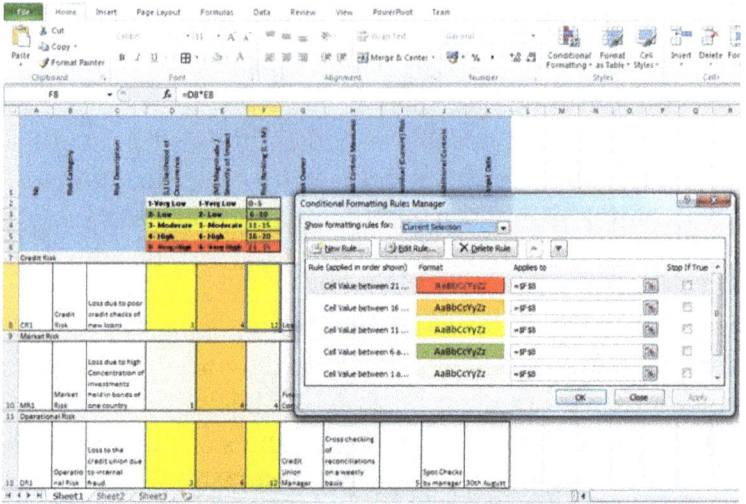

Figure 3: Using Conditional Formatting in a Risk Register

Figure 3 provides an example of a risk register in a spreadsheet, with conditional formatting to aid the review process.

For each risk listed in the risk register, both probability and impact are measured on a "1 to 5" scale. Probability can be applied as a series of percentages (e.g., 1 could be 2%, 2 could be 5%, 3 could be 15%, 4 could be 25% and 5 could be 50%). Impact can be connected to financial items unique to a firm (e.g., the amount of total reserves beyond the required amount to be held by a firm – if the amount in 2020 is about $1,000,000 then 1 could be $20,000, 2 could be $50,000, 3 could be $100,000, 4 could be $100,000 and 5 would be $500,000.)

The scales for likelihood of probability or impact may vary from organization to organization. The important point is to choose a scale that suits firm and apply it consistently.

N°	CR1	MR1	OR1	BS1	GR1
RISK CATEGORY	Credit Risk	Market Risk	Operational Risk	Business Model/ Stratgic Risk	Governance risk
RISK DESCRIPTION	Loss due to poor credit checks of new loans	Loss due to high concentration of investments held in bonds of one country	Loss to the credit union due to internal fraud	Credit Union does not meer the targets in the strategic plan	Lack of evidence of board meetings being kept
(L)LIKEHOOD OF OCCURRENCE	3	1	3	4	4
(M)MAGNITUDE/ SEVERITY OF	4	4	4	2	3
RISK RANTING (LxM)	12	4	12	8	12
RISK OWNER	Loan Officer	Finanncial Controller	Credit Union Manager	Credit Union Manager	Board Secretary
RISK CONTROL MEASURES	New Credit Scoring System	Engage with advisors to place 33% of bond port-folio With another country	Cross Checking of reconciliations on a weekly basis	Balalnced Score Card Sysmen to be put in place to link goals to measuremenst	Board meeting minutes to be kep in an agreed format on the network drive
RESIDUAL (CURRENT) RISK	8	2	5	4	4
ADDITIONAL CONTROLS	Credit Committe meeting	Monthly Investment Committee Meeting	Spot Checks by manager	Quarterly review of the strategic plan	Minutes of meetings reviewed and approved at meetings
TARGET DATE	30th March	30th September	30th August	30th June	25th May

Very Low	0-5
Low	6-10
Moderate	11-15
High	16-20
Very High	21-25

Figure 4: Sample Risks in a Risk Register Template

Figure 4 provides samples of risks in a risk register. This book could spend a considerable amount on this topic but it is sufficient for now to consider the role of the risk register in recording and communication of the inherent and residual risks, and the controls amd systems that drives the difference between the two of these.

Risk Management Policy and Overview

Risk management is not just the role of the risk manager or the risk management function. Management and the board of directors also have a role.

The role of the board is primarily one of oversight as ultimately the board can be accountable to shareholders or other such stakeholders. Senior management and board members should actively engage in the oversight process. The board of directors plays an active part in areas such as policy design and selecting a risk appetite. Therefore, the full board should have some knowledge and oversight of the firm's key risks.

Management and the board should lead by example and ensure accountability. This means they should put into practice the firm's values. This is sometimes called the "tone from the top".

The board of directors, in conjunction with its committees, can oversee risk management programs by:

- Focusing attention on critical risk areas, with a regular review of the firm's risk register and the risk profile of the firm and taking action in respect of any risks that have been escalated.
- Taking top level ownership and support of the risk management agenda and the firm's overall risk management policy.
- Working with management to incorporate leading practices (e.g., protocols for investigating complaints and internal reporting) and holding management to account for complying with and operating the organizational risk management processes.
- Setting the "tone at the top", both internally within the firm and externally within the wider community.

Two items aid in this work – the firm's risk policy and risk appetite – or indeed in a larger firm risk policies and risk appetites.

The risk management policy sets out the overall strategy of the firm regarding risk management. It defines risk management roles and responsibilities and sets out the approach to risk management that should be followed. The policy should be reviewed on an annual basis to ensure that risk management activities and the overall risk management approach are in line with current best practice. Importantly, it gives the firm the opportunity to identify the risk priorities and make sure that appropriate attention is paid to the significant risks.

An annual review of the policy focuses management and board attention on the issue of risk management and helps them to understand that risk management is a dynamic activity that requires constant review.

The format of a risk policy can vary between firms. It can be a short document giving a brief outline of the main structures and roles for the organization of risk management or a long and more detailed document.

The risk appetite is the level of risk that a firm is prepared to seek, accept, or tolerate. One of the main tasks of the board in relation to risk appetite is the consideration of the nature and categories of risk it regards as acceptable for the firm to bear. The board has a responsibility to define the high-level risk appetite of the firm.

The board should maintain a view of the firm and its culture through observation and consultation with management.

To influence culture and tone, the board can:

- Review metrics and key performance indicators (KPIs) with respect to the firm's compliance with law and policy and regarding risk incidences (e.g., reporting on the number of non-compliance issues, operational risk incidents).
- Maintain an understanding of the compliance monitoring, testing, and issue resolution process.
- Assess the adequacy of management's response to specific issues and areas of internal control weakness.

1.5 Summary

You should now be familiar with risk, risk management, some of the different types of risk, and how they can be combined together with elements such as the risk policy and risk register to create a risk management system – something that is not to be confused with commercial software packages that aid with the running of the risk management system. The role of the risk manager should be understood. Finally, there should be an understanding of risk across the financial services industry.

Chapter 2: Market Risk

2.1 Introduction

Market risk relates to changes in values and prices in various market types including the foreign exchange and commodities markets.

To manage market risk, market participants use a number of techniques including value-at-risk (VAR) and stress testing. These techniques will be explored in this chapter.

Interest rate risk is also addressed in this chapter and can be taken as a sub category of market risk. Understanding this relationship will aid in understanding items like the global bond market.

2.2 Market Risk

Market Risk

Market Risk is the risk that the value of investments and their related cash flows will decrease or increase. This risk can arise from fluctuations in both the values of and income from assets or changes in interest rate, exchange rates between currencies, and other such items.

Market risk can be divided into four major types:

- Interest rate risk is risk that the value of a fixed-income security such as a bond will increase or decrease because of changes to market interest rates;

- Equity price risk relates to the volatility of stock prices and indices. The general market risk of equity refers to the sensitivity of an equity instrument or portfolio value to a change in the level of broad stock market indices;
- Foreign exchange risk arises from positions in foreign currency denominated assets and liabilities leading profits or losses as measured in local currency. These positions may arise from a position taking by a trader in a certain currency or from business operations that involve a foreign currency. This is a major risk exposure of corporations involved in international trade; and,
- Commodity risk is the threat of changes to a commodity price that may have an impact on future market value and income.

Participants and Products

The participants in the financial markets can be divided in various ways including "investor" versus "speculator" or "institutional" versus "retail". The participants are considered to be buy side vs sell side. The "buy side" tends to refer to firms that purchase securities, and can include investment managers, pension funds, and hedge funds. The "sell side" refers to firms that issue, sell, or trade securities, and can include investment banks, advisory firms, and corporations.

Many firms will find themselves on the sell side when they are looking to raise funds for new business. The financial markets are used to attract funds from those on the buy side to be provided to those on the sell side such as corporations. This allows corporations to finance their operations and growth and thus to make a profit that is shared with investors on the buy side.

In addition, the money markets allow firms to borrow funds on a short-term basis, while capital markets allow corporations to gain long-term funding to support expansion. Without financial markets, firms would have difficulty finding investors. Intermediaries such as investment banks help in this process and receive their own income in return.

Within these markets products can include:

- Financials assets such as currency, deposit accounts, and negotiable instruments, or longer term instruments such as bonds, common stock, or long-term notes.
- Derivative instruments where worth is derived from the value and characteristics of an underlying entity. The instruments can be exchange-traded derivatives and over-the-counter (OTC) derivatives. Some of the more common derivatives include options, forwards, futures, swaps, and variations of these. An example is an option which gives the right but not the obligation to buy an underlying asset at a certain price in the future.

2.3 Taking Market Risk Beyond VAR and Stress Testing

Two methods for the management of market risk include value at risk (VAR) and stress testing. The first, value at risk, or VAR, is more objective, data driven, and methodological than stress testing. Stress testing is more subjective and judgement-based, but can still include a large amount of data. VAR has become a popular means of measuring market risk but has come under some scrutiny in recent years.

Value at Risk (VAR)

Market risk is typically measured using a value at risk (VAR) methodology. VAR is well established as a risk management technique and relates to a question for any investor: What is the most that could be lost in a single day of trading?

In more detail, the question is What is the most I could lose on my portfolio in a single day with 95% confidence that I will not lose more than that amount?"

At its simplest, one way a market risk manager calculates this is with historic returns from their portfolio for a certain time period. These returns are arranged in a histogram showing the number of days certain losses or gains were made. See figure 5 for an example of a distribution of daily returns.

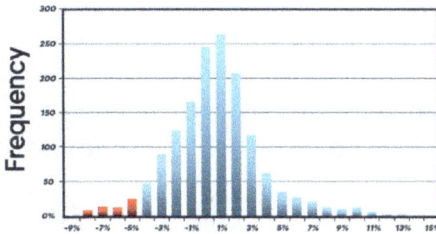

Figure 5: Example Distribution of Daily Returns

If a firm has an investment with a daily VAR of €1,000 at the 99 percent confidence level, we mean that the realized daily losses from the position will on average be higher than €1,000 on only one day every 100 trading days, that is two to three days each year. This is a useful measure as it is relatively easily understood and can be used to set bounds on what can be invested in by a firm. If the VAR for an investment is found to be €1,000,000 for a firm with €10,000,000 in assets, then a decision may be made to back out of the investment.

VAR has come under some criticism in recent years, mainly as some claimed it could estimate the risks of rare market events and give false confidence. However, if there is an understanding of the detail behind VAR and importantly that the figure produced is not a worst case scenario (i.e.,the 99% confidence in the example above was €1,000 but the 99.5% confidence could be €500,000), then VAR is still a useful tool.

VAR may be used for a variety of asset classes including equities and bonds to allow a convenient, yet powerful, measure of the risk for the investment portfolio of any firm.

Stress Testing

In finance, a stress test is a simulation designed to determine the ability of financial instruments or financial institutions to deal with an economic crisis.

A stress test may involve the following stresses:

- What happens if house prices decline by a certain percent?
- What happens if oil prices rise by a certain amount per barrel?
- What happens if the unemployment rate rises to a certain percentage in the following 3 years?
- What happens if interest rates fall by at least a certain percentage?
- What happens if an institutions income falls by a certain amount that year?

In recent years, financial regulators and similar bodies have implemented liquid capital levels as compared to a firm's overall holdings as a regulatory requirement. The focus has been to ensure that there are adequate levels of capital to cover possible losses incurred during extreme market events.

Methods of stress testing can include:

- Historical Analysis Stress Test: The financial instruments or financial institutions are run through a simulation based on a previous crisis. Examples of historical crises include the stock market crash of October 1987, the dot com crash of the early 2000s, and the financial crisis of 2007-08. A subset of these crises could also be used (e.g., the Nevada Housing Market during the financial crisis of 2007-08).

- Achilles Heel Method Stress Test: This approach examines an existing portfolio to find its vulnerabilities and then creates stress scenarios that fully exploit these vulnerabilities.
- Forward Looking Marco Stress Test: This approach involves modelling the impact on capital and other balance sheet items of financial institutions to changes in key macroeconomic and financial variables.

Stress testing can be enhanced using scenario design. With scenario design, the risk manager selects from a range of scenarios and related data. Usually three scenarios are used such as baseline, adverse, and severely adverse. Examples of these include:

- Baseline: house prices rise by 2%, unemployment falls to 5% and interest rates fall to 1%;
- Adverse: house prices decline by 3%, unemployment rate rises to 9% and interest rates rise to 5%; and,
- Severely adverse: house prices decline by 20%, unemployment rate rises to 18% and interest rise to 10%.

	HOUSING PRICES	UNEMPLOYMENT RATE	INTEREST RATE
Baseline	↑ 2%	↓ 5%	↓ 1%
Adverse	↓ 3%	↑ 9%	↑ 5%
Severely Adverse	↓ 20%	↑ 18%	↑ 10%

Figure N: Sample Scenario Design

Figure 6: Sample scenario design

2.4 Interest Rate Risk and How to Mitigate it

Interest rate risk is the risk that an investment's value will change due to a change in the absolute level of interest rates, in the difference between two rates, or in the shape of the yield curve.

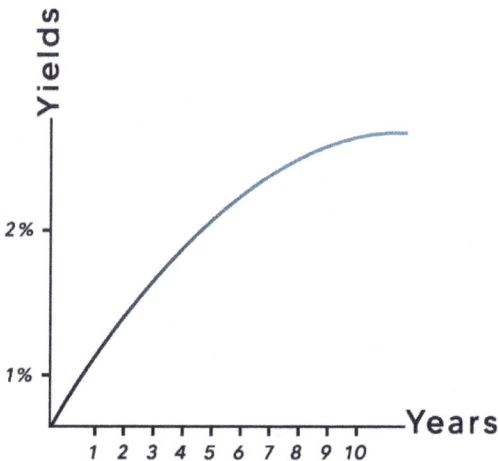

Figure 7: A Typical Yield Curve

Yield curves can be constructed by plotting the return of an investment for increasing durations. The yield curve is a drawing of a curve showing the interest rates across different contract lengths (e.g., 3 month, 3 years, 10 year, etc.) for a debt-based financial instrument. As longer investments are seen to be riskier due to the risk of default increasing over time, the related return is usually greater and thus a typical yield curve will have a curve showing increasing return over a longer period.

A normal yield curve, such as the one in figure 7, is one in which longer-term maturity bonds have a higher yield compared to shorter-term bonds. An inverted yield curve is one in which the shorter-term yields are higher than the longer-term yields, which can be a sign of upcoming recession as governments and other lenders try to adjust interest rates to manage the economy.

Bond and Interest Rate Risk

Bonds are loans raised by borrowers from investors at fixed rates of interest for fixed periods of years. Borrowers are typically governments, government agencies, or corporations. Typically the borrower, or issuer of the bond, undertakes to pay the investors a fixed rate of interest each year for the fixed period, and to repay the principal (i.e., the capital amount originally borrowed) when the loan matures at the end of the period.

Bonds are divisible among several investors and are typically denominated in nominal units (for example, of €100 for bonds when issued by Eurozone borrowers). The fixed rate of interest refers to the rate payable annually per €100 and is called the "coupon".

A bond is identified by its fixed rate of interest (or coupon), its issuer, and its redemption date. As an example, "4.50 percent Treasury Bond 2015" would mean that the coupon on this bond is 4.5%. The issuer, in this case the Irish government, will make an annual interest payment of 4.5% to the investor in the bond up to and including the maturity date. On the maturity date in 2015, the Irish Government will pay the holder €100 per €100 nominal held of the bond.

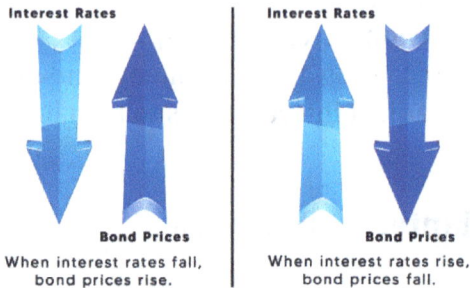

Figure 8: The Relationship between Bonds and Interest Rates

For example, the example 4.5% bond is worth more if interest rates decrease since the bondholder receives a fixed rate of return relative to the market, which is offering a lower rate of return as a result of the decrease in rates. However, if interest rates rise – for example to 6%, then our example bond is worth less as better returns will be available in the market.

Managing Interest Rate Risk

Interest rates can expose firms to risk. A historical example is the savings and loan banks in the United States in the 1980s and 1990s. These institutions had a business model of accepting deposits from their customers and in turn using these funds to make loans including car loans and home mortgages. Due to increases in the discount rate charged by the U.S. Federal Reserve System, the savings and loans found themselves on the wrong side of interest rate risk. They had issued long-term loans at fixed interest rates that were lower than the interest rate at which they could borrow and taken on deposits, which paid higher interest rates than the rate at which they could borrow. This resulted in over a thousand of the over three thousand savings and loan institutions failing. Costs to the U.S. taxpayers as a result were in the hundreds of billions of dollars.

There are two ways interest rate risk can be managed: through the management of the balance sheet and the use of derivatives.

Through careful management of the asset/liability mix on a balance sheet, interest rate risk to which firms are exposed can be managed.

Interest rate risk is managed by the use of common derivatives including forwards, options, and swaps. Traditionally, derivatives were traded over the counter but there has been a recent push for them to be traded on exchanges. An example of how derivatives can be used is if a swap is entered into, a firm may have a commitment to pay out on a variable rate and to be paid on a fixed rate. A contract can be entered into the swap, for example, the variable rate for a fixed rate – refereed to below as a swap.

The most popular derivative instruments for interest rate risk management are:

- Forwards: A forward is a contract between two parties to buy or sell an asset at a specified future time at an agreed-on price. The price is agreed on well in advance of the settlement date. The most important forward for interest rate risk is the forward rate agreement (FRA), a forward contract in which the determinant of gain or loss is an interest rate. Payments are calculated based on a notional principal amount and paid at intervals determined by the parties. FRAs are always settled in cash and they are settled net, which means the parties determine how they might have benefited or lost due to the interest rate change and pay the difference. FRAs allow institutional borrowers and lenders to protect themselves if exposed to interest rate risk.

- Futures: A futures contract is similar to a forward but since it is standardized and trades on an exchange, it reduces risk for counterparties. There is a reduction of default and liquidity risk due to the inclusion of the exchange.
- Swaps: An interest rate swap is essentially a series of FRAs, an agreement between counterparties to exchange sets of future cash flows. The most common type of interest rate swap is a plain vanilla swap, which involves one party paying a fixed interest rate and receiving a floating rate, and the other party paying a floating rate and receiving a fixed rate.
- Options: Interest rate management options are option contracts for which an underlying security is a debt obligation. These instruments are useful for protecting the counterparties involved in a floating-rate loan. A grouping of interest rate calls is called an interest rate cap; a combination of interest rate puts is called an interest rate floor. A swaption (swap option) is an option to enter a swap.

2.5 Summary

You should now be familiar with a series of related items that are important for the risk management officer in any financial services firm and indeed in any firm that may be involved in any interaction with the financial markets.

Chapter 3: Credit Risk

3.1 Introduction

It can be argued that credit risk is the most important of all risks for banks. Without extending credit to customers, a bank is without a purpose. However, all firms can be exposed to credit risk, whether or not they are in financial services. If credit risk is considered to be the risk of financial loss arising from an obligor, borrower, or counterparty who fails to meet its obligations in accordance with agreed term, then the relevance of credit risk for firms beyond the banking world is understood.

This chapter examines what credit risk is, how it is managed, and defines the role of the participants including a credit rating agency. The focus of this chapter is on retail credit risk, that is the risk in extending credit to individual borrowers. However commercial risk management, the extension of credit to business borrowers, is briefly explored in the risk assessment part of the chapter.

3.2 What is Credit Risk?

Credit risk is best understood as the potential that a borrower or counterparty will fail to meet the obligations in the terms agreed to between them and the lender. For most financial services organizations like banks, loans are the largest and most typical source of credit risk. However, all kinds of firms may extend risk to their customers.

The most likely appearance of credit risk is when the borrower fails to make the agreed payments to the lender. This may result in the lender losing the interest on the loan or the principle of the loan. This in turn can result in disrupted cash flows affecting the firm's asset liability management and increased provisions against these potential bad debts.

Credit risk may be considered to have three sub-categories:

- Inherent credit risk is the credit risk that arises anytime a firm's funds are extended or in some exposed to another party. A prudent lender will first assess the credit worthiness of this party before the funds are extended.
- Credit concentration risk is when a lender may be exposed to a certain set of borrowers to such a degree that the potential losses are large enough to affect the lender's operations or changes the organization's risk profile. Some lenders may say that they "know their customers" and thus see lending to a certain market as a strength. However, diversification in who is lent to can be a form of risk mitigation against credit concentration risk.
- Credit control relates to how a lender reacts when a payment is missed and how the situation may be resolved or the funds recovered.

Related to all of this is the concept that the higher the credit risk being taken on by the lender, the higher the interest rate that the lender will be asked to pay. This again relates to the risk versus reward discussion in the earlier part of this book.

Assessing Credit Risk

For loans to individuals, credit risk can be assessed through processes such as credit scoring. Prior to extending credit through a loan the lender will obtain information about the borrower. Typically, this might include the borrower's income, existing borrowings, any arrears they may have on other borrowings, and whether they rent or own a home. Figure 9 provides an example of a credit score model for retail risk.

A standard formula is applied to the information to produce a number, which is called a credit score. Based upon the credit score, the lender will decide whether to extend credit. Over the last few decades this process has become standardized.

INFORMACION	ANSWER AND RELATED SCORE			
Years in Job	0-12 Months 5 Points	1-2 Years 10 Points	2-5 Years 15 Points	5+ Years 20 Points
Own or Rent	Own 40 Points	Rent 20 Points		
Other Banking	ATM Acconunt 22 Points	Savings 25 Points	Both 34 Points	
Credit Cards	Yes 30 Points	NO 11 Points		
Occupation	Retired 20 Points	Professional 30 Points	Sales 30 Points	Others 35 Points
Age of Borrower	18 to 25 25 Points	26 to 40 15 Points	41 to 60 30 Points	61+ 25 Points
Worst Credit Reference	Poor -30 Points	Fair -15 Points	Satisfactory 0 Points	Good +10 Points

Figure 9: An Example Credit Score Model for Retail Risk

The gathering of the data for these models and ensuring it is complete and accurate is a major part of this exercise. Also, the managing of exceptions around the credit scoring process is important. It is possible that credit scoring may show approval for a customer who in fact will go on to default on the loan with the opposite also being possible. A person who would have met the terms of the loan and made their payments in full and on-time could have been rejected.

Understanding the underlying process of assessing and approving loans helps with ensuring that these errors do not happen in a prudent organization.

Managing Credit Risk

There are other considerations for a lender in how they manage their credit risk besides assessment. These considerations are part of the overall credit lifecycle, as shown in figure 10.

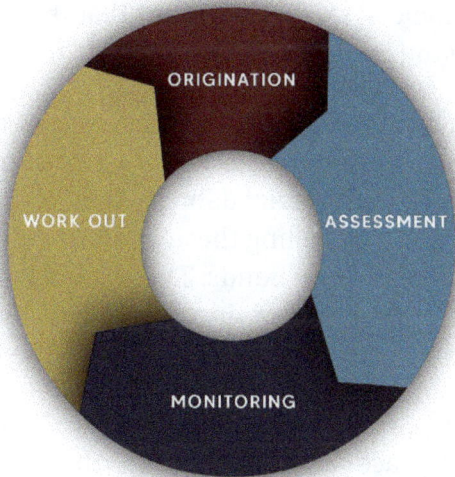

Figure 10: The Credit Lifecycle

Within the origination and assessment stages is risk-based pricing where, as with the risk versus reward note earlier in the chapter, the lender can charge a higher interest rate to borrowers who are more likely to default. This will allow a better overall return for the portfolio of loans as it takes into account the cost of a loan becoming non-performing. Related to the management of the portfolio of loans, lenders face a high degree of concentration risk if they lend to a certain kind of borrower or to borrowers in a certain area. Lenders can reduce this risk by diversifying the borrower pool and by offering other kinds of loan products.

Credit insurance or credit derivatives can be used by lenders to hedge their credit risk by purchasing contracts to transfer the risk from the lender to the seller (insurer) in exchange for a payment. The most common credit derivative is the credit default swap which is a financial swap agreement that the seller will compensate the buyer in the event of a loan default.

Lenders can also transfer some of their credit risk through securitization. This is the practice of pooling various types of contractual debt, such as mortgages or credit card debt, and selling these pools of debt as securities that resemble bonds. The principal and interest on the debt, underlying the security, is paid back to the various investors regularly via the interest payments being made on the loans.

Both of these practices result in issues that led to the recent financial crisis of 2007-08. For example, lenders were less worried about the potential quality of a borrower if they knew they would be selling the loan onwards as part of a pool of debt in a securitization deal.

The next stages in the credit lifecycle are monitoring and work out. Despite the best efforts in credit risk assessment before the loan was made, there may be issues with the payment of the interest and indeed the entire loan. If this should occur, there can be two main effects on the lender. First, the lender must make provisions for the potential loss on the loan. In addition, the lender must work to try and reclaim any funds from delinquent borrowers. It is at this point that good operational control around the assessment of the credit risk of the borrower and the making of the loan to them becomes important. Any information that was gathered should be well evidenced to ensure that the information gathered was in no way misrepresented by the borrower. Any covenants written into the loan should be properly documented and signed off, and any collateral should be properly secured. Thus, if the loan is not recoverable, some of the funds may be recovered via the collateral.

3.3 Credit and Sub Prime

The purchase of a property as a home can be one of the largest purchases in a person's life. It can also make a good investment with house prices in most markets usually increasing throughout the last few decades. But purchasing a property can also be an expensive time; some markets will expect a house price to be a multiple of the purchaser's annual income. Few people will have this amount of funding available as a lump sum and saving up could take many years.

This is where a mortgage may be useful. A mortgage is a loan in which property is used as collateral. The borrower enters into an agreement with the lender wherein the borrower receives cash upfront then makes payments over a set time span until the borrower pays back the lender in full plus an agreed-upon interest rate.

Mortgages can either be funded through by a bank through deposit taking or through the capital markets using securitization. Securitization is the process of pooling various types of contractual debt and selling the related cash flows to investors as securities. Relevant here is taking and creating mortgage-backed securities (MBS) that can be sold to investors in various denominations.

Securitization has several advantages; the first is that banks can move their loans off their balance sheet and sources funds to allow them to offer further mortgage to more customers. This can be viewed as reducing the risk being held by the bank. In addition, investors can benefit from investment in property, without having to be involved in the loan origination process. Finally, it is viewed that this allows the risk related to mortgages to be diversified across the financial markets.

The way in which the related investments are structured was also meant to help with risk management.

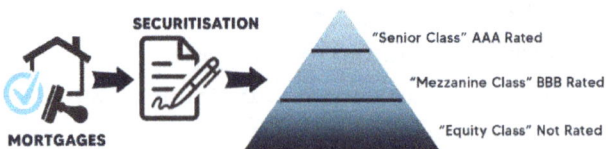

Figure 11: Creating Mortgage-Backed Securities (MBS)

The issued securities are often split into what are called tranches as shown in figure 11. Each tranche has a different level of risk exposure. Firstly, there is generally a senior class of securities. The senior classes have first claim on the cash coming from the underlying mortgages. Next is a mezzanine tranche which receives repayment after the senior class has been repaid. This tranche is riskier and thus a higher interest rate is paid on the mezzanine tranche than on the senior class - again, risk is rewarded. If the underlying mortgages have issues and thus cannot make payments on the securities, the loss is absorbed first by the lower tranches, and the upper-level tranches remain unaffected until the losses exceed the entire amount of the lower tranches. The most junior class, usually called the equity class is the most exposed to payment risk, so with the highest risk, it is paid the highest interest rate. In some cases, this is a special type of instrument which is retained by the originating firm and this allows a potential profit.

Contagion: The Risk Spreads

Throughout the early 2000s, the use of securitization to create mortgage backed securities caused few concerns and grew over time. By the mid- to late- 2000s, a series of events occurred that put these at the heart of the emerging financial crisis of 2007-08. One of these was a desire to originate more mortgages to feed an appetite for more mortgage back securities. With those originating mortgages being rewarded in various forms including commission, some mortgage brokers became less scrupulous about the quality of the mortgages that were being created. Mortgage qualification guidelines became progressively looser passing from a requirement to evidence an ability to repay and proving an ongoing source of income, to what ultimately was known as the "No Income, No Assets, No Job", or NINJA, loans where the borrower did not need to show proof of income or assets to be awarded a mortgage.

Meanwhile, the related securities were being invested in by an increasing type of investor in more diverse locations. This resulted in the odd situation where municipal councils in Europe were invested in securities that ultimately depended on housing markets and mortgages in places like Florida and Nevada in the United States. But with the housing markets in such locations showing good growth, again there was little concern.

Greed Becomes Fear

The US housing market peaked around the mid-2000s and by 2007 investors were became less willing to invest in the related mortgage-backed securities. The true impact of the crisis began to be felt when some of the holdings of the most junior and equity tranche related mortgage securities had to be written down by billions of dollars in value. As financial firms started to realize the extent of both their and others' holdings of these suddenly undesirable investments, the global markets started to enter a period of turmoil.

This reduced trust in the markets and impacted the related liquidity.

The crisis hit a critical point in September 2008 with the failure of investment bank Lehman Brothers, a bailout of the insurance firm AIG, and Merrill Lynch being purchased by Bank of America. Global markets fell and governments and central banks had to intervene to prevent a feared collapse of the global financial system. Central banks purchased trillions of dollars of government debt and troubled assets from banks. It was the largest liquidity injection into the markets, and the largest monetary policy action taken to date.

3.4 Retail and Commercial Credit Risk

Retail credit risk is related to the lending made to consumers (and in some definitions small businesses) such as motor loans, mortgages, and revolving credit lines like overdrafts. The main characteristic of retail credit risk is that it is well-diversified since it is made up of many little exposures. Thus a default by one customer who is a borrower should not threaten the entire lender.

Typically, retail borrowers are financially independent. This is unlike corporate lending which can be concentrated in a particular location or industry. Losses are seen as "predictable" and some retail credit risk can be predicted from changes in behavior of customers such as a minimum payment one month. However, lenders to retail customers are vulnerable to systemic risks (e.g., the recent financial crisis in affected a large part of the retail credit portfolios of lenders).

Commercial credit risk can be a major risk for lenders due to the size and complexity of the related lending. It is possible for lenders to expose themselves to a small set of lenders or to a certain sector. Many banks will develop their own credit rating system to perform a review of a commercial borrower and make a determination on the possibility of default and the possible exposure to the lender if this should happen.

Typical elements of a commercial credit rating system may include:

- Financial Assessment: a review of the borrower to ascertain its financial health.
- Management Assessment: a review of the leadership of the borrower and its day to day management.
- Industry assessment and tier within industry: an assessment of the borrower's industry overall and its success with it.
- Financial statement quality: a review of the accounting and auditing of the borrower.
- Country risk: an assessment of the borrowers economic and political exposures due to its geographic position or markets.
- Loan structure: the loan may be affected by the collateral put in place and any other obligations agreed.
- Cross-check with agency ratings: the assessment made within the lender can be checked against the rating given by external credit rating agencies.

Credit Rating Agencies

External credit rating agencies, firms such as Moody's, Fitch, and S&P, perform an assessment of the credit worthiness of organizations and then publish an opinion on the credit worthiness of a firm seeking to borrow on the markets. The types of ratings published by these firms is shown in figure 12.

FITCH	S&P	MOODY'S		RATING GRADE DESCRIPTION (MOODY'S)
AAA	AAA	Aaa		MINIMAL CREDIT RISK
AA+ AA AA-	AA+ AA AA-	Aa1 Aa2 Aa3	INVESTMENT GRADE	Very low credit risk
A+ A A-	A+ A A-	A1 A2 A3	INVESTMENT GRADE	Low credit risk
BBB+ BBB BBB-	BBB+ BBB BBB-	Baa1 Baa2 Baa3	INVESTMENT GRADE	Moderate credit risk
BB+ BB BB-	BB+ BB BB-	Ba1 Ba2 Ba3	SPECULATIVE GRADE	Substantial credit risk
B+ B B-	B+ B B-	B1 B2 B3	SPECULATIVE GRADE	High credit risk
CCC+ CCC CCC-	CCC+ CCC CCC-	Caa1 Caa2 Caa3	SPECULATIVE GRADE	Very high credit risk
CC C	CC C	Ca	SPECULATIVE GRADE	In or near default, with possibility of recovery
DD DD D	SD D	C	SPECULATIVE GRADE	In default, with little chance of recovery

Figure 12: Commercial Credit Rating Agency Ratings

Credit rating agencies typically assign letter grades to indicate ratings (i.e., a credit rating scale ranging from AAA (the best rating) down to C and D). A debt instrument such as a bond with a rating below BBB- is considered a speculative grade or a junk bond. This rating can be related back to the investment policy of a firm which may declare that they invest in bonds that are of an investment grade as defined by the rating agencies. Related to the relationship noted earlier about risk versus reward, a bond with a good investment rating is seen as less risky and thus will reward an investor with a lower return on their investment.

The accuracy of agency ratings is assessed by reviewing multi-year rating transition matrices that show the probability of a firm migrating from one rating to another in a year, as shown in figure 13. A AAA-rated item is seen to have a very high probability of being at that rating or perhaps something nearby like AA rated in another year. The converse is that low-rated item at a rating such as CCC is quite likely to have defaulted in the coming year.

ORIGINAL RATING	PROBABILITY OF MIGRATING TO RATING BY YEAR EN (%)							
	AAA	AA	A	BBB	BB	B	CCC	Default
AAA	93.66	5.83	0.40	0.08	0.03	0.00	0.00	0.00
AA	0.66	91.72	6.94	0.49	0.06	0.09	0.02	0.01
A	0.07	2.25	91.76	5.19	0.49	0.20	0.01	0.04
BBB	0.03	0.25	4.83	89.26	4.44	0.81	0.16	0.22
BB	0.03	0.07	0.44	6.67	83.31	7.47	1.05	0.98
B	0.00	0.10	0.33	0.46	5.77	84.19	3.87	5.30
CCC	0.16	0.00	0.31	0.93	2.00	10.74	63.96	21.94
Default	0.00	0.00	0.00	0.00	0.00	0.00	0.00	100.00

Figure 13: Commercial Credit Rating Agency Cumulative Default Statistics

3.5 Summary

Credit risk is something that almost all firms need to accept – it is part of the core business of banks and cannot be avoided for any firm that extends credit to others, even if it is just via the sales process.

By adopting some of the practices explored in this chapter, credit risk can be at least reduced.

Chapter 4: Liquidity Risk and Asset Liability Management

4.1 Introduction

The ability to meet cashflows is important for both financial and non-financial firms. This is a type of liquidity risk and is the next risk category that will be explored in this chapter.

Examples of liquidity risk include loss of existing funding, new lending or investments, and timing mismatches between asset maturities and liability cash flow. It is on this last item that this chapter will spend some additional time – how a firm's management of assets and liabilities aids in managing liquidity and other risks.

4.2 What is Liquidity Risk?

Fundamentally, there are two type of liquidity risk:

- Market liquidity: Risk that an item cannot be sold to another market participant due to a lack of liquidity in the market. This is more relevant to investments and market risk.
- Funding liquidity: Risk that liabilities cannot be met when they are due or can be met only at a cost that is a great disadvantage to the market participant.

Market liquidity is itself a significant area, and relates to markets, volumes of trading, and how prices are affected by the amount of a security being sold in a market. During the 2007-08 crisis, some financial markets seized, resulting in the inability to determine market prices. The focus is funding liquidity and how this affects the ability of a bank to meet obligations as they fall.

A best practice includes holding a pool of liquid assets that cushions against unexpected obligations or a sudden inability to source funds to meet expected obligations. After the 2007-08 crisis, this practice became a regulatory requirement and banks were expected to hold a fraction of their balance sheet in the form of liquid assets. The regulation expects that enough short-term liquid assets are held to match short-term, upcoming liabilities. This fraction is known as the liquidity ratio and is calculated by dividing liquid assets by short-term liabilities.

In a situation in which this liquidity pool must be called on, market liquidity risk and credit risk might come into play. Unexpected losses in the markets might result in an asset sell-off, driving prices down and resulting in yet more sell-offs. As more and more sellers chase a decreasing number of buyers, or in an extreme case, no buyers emerge at any price, what in normal times was a promising liquidity pool can be found to be of little use.

There can also be a contagion effect; if illiquid assets cannot be sold, a firm that needs to sell something might be forced to sell liquid assets instead, resulting in a fall in price of goods and liquid securities, and supply exceeding demand. As markets fall, confidence in market participants might also fall, resulting in reluctance of participants to lend to one another.

Sources of funding can influence overall liquidity management. A simple measurement of funding liquidity is the stability of funding sources. As described in section 2.2, traditionally, banks fund activities such as lending through deposits from customers. Over time, banks started to use other sources of funding such as certificates of deposits, federal funds, foreign deposits, repos, and many others to fund activities. These alternative funding sources have sometimes been placed under the title of wholesale funding.

Figure 14: Funding options for banks

Traditional deposits have the advantage over other funding sources as being relatively inexpensive and easily available if there is an existing deposit business for the bank. However, commercially focused banks might not have this ready source of funding and traditional banks expanding the business might also start to depend on wholesale funding.

The advantages of wholesale funding are:

- Availability: In normal times, there is plenty of funding available or being requested. Thus, a firm can enter the market and either fund deficits or earn on funding surpluses.

- Duration: Since the circumstance of a firm being in surplus or deficit can change daily, wholesale funding is ideal. In interbank markets in which banks lend to one another for short periods, loans are usually for maturities of one week or less, with the majority being overnight.
- Business model: Wholesale funding allows access to funding that could not normally be accessed as easily or quickly if traditional deposits were used.

One contributing factor to the 2007-08 financial crisis was firms lending to one another. Financial firms lending to one another is a major source of funding and is a good example of the advantages and disadvantages of such funding with low volumes in this market. In the years leading up to the crisis, banks took advantage of the availability and flexibility of the market to develop their business model and increase their balance sheets. However, when there was a perceived increase in counterparty risk between parties, some participants found it increasingly difficult and expensive to source their funding.

Since the duration of many of the funding arrangements was very short (as short as overnight arrangements), any perceived or real issue with market participants could result in the firm suddenly being unable to meet their funding requirements at the end of the day. Banks that normally had large surpluses to lend into interbank markets were now less willing to risk this money with some of their usual counterparties and the banks started to hold back from the markets.

With a decrease in available funding, banks started to hoard liquidity in anticipation of future shortages. The results of this were:

- A vast decrease in transaction volumes and thus liquidity in the markets;
- An increase in the price of funds that were available; and
- More demand for a smaller pool of funding that resulted in higher prices.

Banks whose funding had a majority of less stable funding found themselves entering a liquidity crisis.

4.3 Asset Liability Management

Some causes of the 2007-08 financial crisis related to poor management of assets and liabilities on a firm's balance sheet. In particular, to the funding of a bank's business model. In this section, asset liability management through a bank's balance sheet is introduced, the objectives for asset liability management and how there might be competing demands between making a good return versus interest rate or liquidity risk is discussed.

Asset liability management (ALM) is the practice of matching and sometimes deliberately mismatching the assets and liabilities on an organization's balance sheet, and thus affecting income and value related to these assets and liabilities. For banks, this is typically the practice of managing assets such as loans and liabilities, including deposits on balance sheets and interest-related income.

Mismatches drive the net worth and profitability of a bank and mismatches also create risks. These mismatches might be between the term of loans (banks typically borrow short-term and lend long-term) or interest rates on items like loans and deposits. The complexity of the relationship between assets and liabilities is driven by the action of some borrowers being able to take the option of cutting short their loans to take advantage of better rates of borrowing and the impact of related changes to interest rates to items on a bank's balance sheet. On the other side of such transactions, borrowers may be able to take advantage of options in savings products. Finally, there is the choice and availability of both fixed and floating rates of interest to add to the complexity of ALM.

These elements affect the net worth and profitability of banks. If interest rates fall, a bank might benefit since shorter maturity deposits soon cost less for the bank to pay out, while the bank continues to benefit from the still higher interest rate on longer-maturity loans. However, a rise in interest rates has the opposite effect, and could lower the net worth of a bank. In addition, rise in rates will exacerbate mismatch risk from both sides of the balance sheet. As an example, loans extend as prepayments fall while retail deposit durations typically shorten as depositors withdraw funds to take advantage of higher rates.

Although matching of these items continues, the bank has to ensure it has sufficient liquidity on hand to maintain such gaps. For example, liquidity in the form of cash might be needed if deposits are suddenly withdrawn by customers due to a change in liquidity rates.

Introduction to Gaps

For liquidity risk, the major items to be managed are gaps or unresolved mismatches between assets and liabilities. These gaps can be between cash flows to be paid out and received on the interest-bearing items on the balance sheet, or in the gap between the timings of these cash flows. Figure 15 provides an example of a firm's payments coming due on loans and expected deposits. Fluctuations in the interest income or expenditure could be due to interest-related asset and liabilities coming due or changes in the interest being paid or received for each item.

MONTH	INTEREST INCOME	INTEREST EXPENDITURE	CUMULATIVE TOTAL
JANUARY	€5,000	€10,000	(€5,000)
FEBRUARY	€5,000	€10,000	(€10,000)
MARCH	€5,000	€0	(€5,000)
APRIL	€5,000	€5,000	(€5,000)
MAY	€5,000	€0	(€0)
JUNE	€5,000	€0	(€5,000)

Figure 15: Sample cash flow for a firm

If the bank cannot fund the Cumulative Total loss of €10,000 shown in the month of February through other means, the bank will be unable to maintain its business long enough to benefit from the Cumulative Total profit of €5,000 by the end of June.

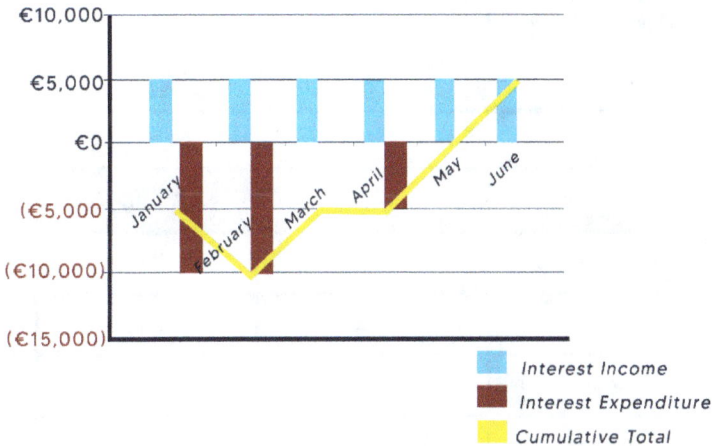

Figure 16: Sample cash flow for a firm in chart form

Figure 16 provides a forecasted view of the firm's cash flow. If the firm views the cashflow as a forecast at the start of the year in January, it might choose to adjust its business model to bring in more interest income earlier in the year, or find a way to adjust its business model to bring in more income.

A Banking Example

To get a better understanding of ALM, figures 17 and 18 provide the most common financial statements used by a bank to aid the understanding of the financial performance of a bank and its business model.

INCOME STATEMENT - WESTERN CLIFF BANCK
All Figure in Mollions of Dollars

	Year Ending 31 Dec 2021	Year Ending 31 Dec 2020
Revenue		
Interest Income	487	523
Interest Expense	273	274
Net Income Interest	214	249
Non-interest Income	219	165
Total Revenue	433	414
Expense		
Loan Loss Provision	50	51
Non-interest Expense	354	345
Total Expense	404	396
Income Before Taxes	29	18
Taxes	6	4
Net Income	23	14

Figure 17: Income statement for a generic bank

Figure 17 provides a simple income statement for Western Cliff Bank, a generic bank. The income statement summarizes the revenues and expenses generated by the bank over a reporting period. The format and content for a bank is usually different from that seen with other types of enterprises since there is a split between interest-related revenue and expenses, and such activities are much more common on a bank's income statement.

Relevant items for ALM from figure 17 include:

- Interest Income: This is income received from assets on the balance sheet of the bank. For a bank, this is the most direct link between the income earned on loans being made to customers or income earned on items on the balance sheet such as bonds or funds held in interest earning accounts. More detailed income statements break this line down further to show subcategories such as interest income on loans, interest earning investments, etc.
- Interest expenses: This is the cost to the bank for items such as interest on customer deposits and relate to the liability side of a bank's balance sheet. On a typical income statement, this line is broken down into further subcategories such as interest on deposits, deposit accounts offered to customers, etc.
- Net Interest Income (NII): Net interest income is interest income minus the interest expense. An important measure of the success of a bank to generate profits through interest rate risk.
- Non-interest Income: This is revenue earned from other activities in a bank such as investment banking and trading, and is important for ALM in banking.

Figure 17 shows the bank's "net income" increased to 23m in 2021 as compared to 14m in 2020. Between the previous and current year ends, there are some interesting patterns emerging in the revenue of this bank.

"Interest income" related to assets such as loans paid less interest income in the year ending 2021 (487m) than the previous year ending 2020 (523m). The "interest expense" from activities such as deposit taking also decreased (273m in 2021 from 274m in 2020). The result is in a decrease in the "net interest income" by 14% from the previous year.

$$(214 - 249) / 249 = -0.1405 \text{ or } -14\%$$

If further examination of the bank's interest income were to find that deposits increased or that the interest expected to be paid on these deposits in percentage terms increased while loans or the interest paid in from them had not, we would have concern about the sustainability of the lending/deposit business model of this bank.

As it is, the non-interest income on items such as trading has increased significantly from the previous year (219m in 2021 as compared to 165m in 2020). This increase in non-interest income allowed the bank to remain profitable. The bank needs to decide if this situation is an accepted part of the bank's business strategy and whether this strategy is sustainable. If neither of these hold true, the bank needs to look at how it can structure the assets and liabilities on its balance sheet to feed into the overall business model and strategy of the bank.

By managing this at a high level in the bank though ALM, this can be achieved more efficiently than by setting up a strategy that could end up pitching deposit takers and loan writers against one another.

BALANCE SHEER AS OF 31 DEC 2021 - WESTERN CLIFF BANK
All Figures in Millons of Dollars

Assets		Liabilities	
Cash at Central Bank	450	Deposits From Institutions	2,400
Debt Securities	1,200	Customer Deposits	3,200
Loans to Banks	400	Debt Securities Issed	90
Loans to Customers	2,900	Other Liabilities	5
Loans to Businesses	1,100	**Total Liabilities**	5,695
Loan Loss Provisions	(50)	**Equity**	
Net Loans	4,350	Preferred Shares	45
Trading Portfolio	125	Equity	450
Fixed Assets	20	Other Reservers	5
Total Assets	6,195	**Liabilities & Equity**	6,195

Figure 18: Balance sheet for a generic bank

Figure 18 provides a simple balance sheet for Western Cliff Bank, a generic bank. A balance sheet is a financial statement that summarizes a bank's assets, liabilities, and shareholders' equity at a given point in time. The format and content for a bank is usually different from that seen with other types of enterprises since the focus here is on banking activities; some items such as a loan loss provision is deducted from items like total loan book.

Relevant items for ALM from figure 18 include:

- Loans to Customers and Businesses: These are the loan-related assets that are expected to earn interest income for the bank. Loans are usually the major assets for a bank and are expected to earn more interest than the securities a bank owns. These loans come with credit risk; if a bank makes bad loans, it will have to write the loans off as losses, and earnings will take a hit. If the bank makes too many of these bad loans, it might find itself insolvent, thus making the structure of these loans important to the business model and management of the bank.
- Debt Securities: These are also interest-earning assets from which a bank earns interest income. A worrying sign for a bank would be an increase in deposits from customers with no corresponding increase in loans, with the resulting surplus having to be placed in this area. Since debt securities earn less than loans, this could result in less overall income and increased costs of maintaining these investments. In this situation, a bank might reject deposits from customers or at least place a cap on such deposits.
- Deposits from Institutions and Customer Deposits: These are the income expense liabilities on which interest must be paid. Customer deposits might be the cheapest source of funds for a bank, and customers might be slow to withdraw deposits, especially if the customer needs to travel to a bank to withdraw funds. Borrowing from institutions such as other banks, insurance companies, and funds is sometimes more costly, but these accounts can be drawn down and returned on more flexible terms. These deposits can be useful when funding a dynamic bank but can be a threat if these sources of

funds are withdrawn when the option to withdraw funds is exercised, as was the case during the 2007-08 crisis.

Management of all these items on the balance sheet is at the heart of asset liability management.

4.4 Post 2008 Crisis Developments

The financial crisis of 2007-08 saw a revisiting of how liquidity risk is measured and managed worldwide.

Basel III

The Basel Accords are a set of recommendations for regulations in the banking industry. Basel I, Basel II, and Basel III were issued by the Basel Committee on Banking Supervision (BCBS). Basel III is the third of these, providing a regulatory standard globally for capital adequacy, stress testing, and market liquidity risk. It was developed as part of the global response to the financial crisis and improves financial regulation and strengthens bank capital requirements by measurement, including increasing bank liquidity.

An initial outline for Basel III was agreed on in 2009 and was brought to more detail into 2010. By the end of 2010, the Basel Committee issued a final version of the new rules, with more details on the definition of regulatory capital in 2011. Related publications that comprise Basel III present a new regime for capital, liquidity, and leverage rules for international banks.

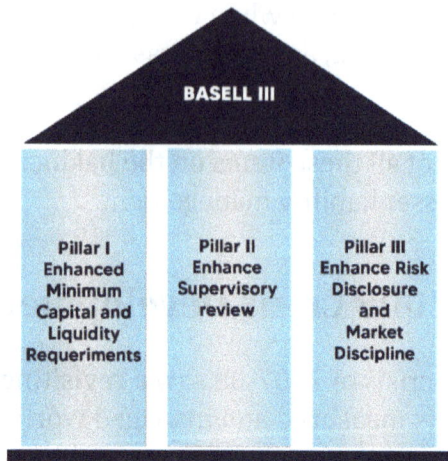

Figure 19: Basel III and the Updated Three Pillars

In response to other elements of the 2007-08 crisis, Basel III introduced a leverage ratio that prevents a repeat of the build-up of leverage in banks. Basel III's leverage ratio is defined as the capital measure (i.e., numerator) divided by the exposure measure (i.e., denominator), expressed as a percentage.

The capital measure is defined as Tier 1 capital, and the minimum leverage ratio is proposed to be 3%. However, further changes might emerge as governments and regulators work toward implementation.

This was scheduled to be introduced from 2013 until 2015; however, implementation was extended repeatedly to 31 March 2019 and as of early 2020 until 1 January 2022.

Liquidity Measures: LCR and NSFR

Changes to bank liquidity and Basel III introduced two new liquidity ratios that ensure banks hold sufficient liquidity for crises in the event wholesale funding markets shut down. These changes encourage a structural shift away from reliance on wholesale funding toward a longer-term and potentially more robust funding strategy. The ratios include a liquidity coverage ratio (LCR), which addresses short-term funding requirements during stress, and the net stable funding ratio (NSFR), which concerns longer-term funding requirements.

Liquidity Coverage Ratio (LCR)

The LCR strengthens a bank's ability to withstand short-term, adverse shocks. The LCR, shown in figure 20, requires banks to hold high-quality liquid assets (e.g., cash, certain types of government bonds, and other liquid securities) to meet net cash outflows over a period of 30 days.

$$\frac{\text{STOCK OF HIGH-QUALITY LIQUID ASSETS}}{\text{NET CASH OUTFLOWS OVER A 30-DAY PERIOD}} \geq 100\%$$

Figure 20: Liquidity Coverage Ratio (LCR)

The LCR was designed with the intention that liquid assets will cover the deficit between cumulative cash inflows and outflows over the 30-day stressed period. When computing net cash outflows, the LCR assumes that during a stressed scenario a proportion of retail deposits may be withdrawn from the bank, resulting in limited access to wholesale funding. The LCR includes the impact of a number of other liquidity risk scenarios, such a credit ratings being downgraded.

Net Stable Funding Ratio (NSFR)

NSFR is a structural measure concerning longer-term funding and encourages banks to have stable funding in place to support operations during a stressed period of one year, on a rolling basis. As shown in figure 21, the result means that the available amount of stable funding must exceed the required amount of stable funding over a one-year period of extended stress. NSFR requires banks to fund long-term, illiquid assets with long-term, stable funding.

$$\frac{\text{AVAILABLE AMOUNT OF STABLE FUNDING}}{\text{REQUIRED AMOUNT OF STABLE FUNDING}} > 100\%$$

Figure 21: Net Stable Funding Ratio (NSFR)

The NSFR looks beyond the 30-day timeframe of the LCR, and reduces the use of short-term funding to finance less-liquid assets. Stable funding sources include capital and long-term debt instruments, retail deposits, and wholesale funding with a maturity of greater than one year, intended to match medium- and long-term lending. Using the NSFR establishes a minimum acceptable amount of stable funding (including long-term debt instruments, retail deposits, and term deposits greater than one year in maturity) based on the liquidity characteristics of an institution's assets and activities over a one-year horizon.

4.5 Summary

Liquidity risk is something that firms need to accept – while some of the focus of this chapter was on banking and asset liability management, any firm that has to fund obligations is exposed to liquidity risk.

Chapter 5: Operational Risk

5.1 Introduction

This chapter introduces operational risk and some ways to mitigate it. Internal controls are introduced and a closer look is provided at how to report on operational risk events and the value in performing a full investigation of more material events.

This is an area where the place of the risk management officer is important – understanding and managing operational risk can have advantages in areas like preventing physical damage to assets, managing IT system outages, and preventing internal and external fraud.

5.2 What is Operational Risk?

Operational risk is referred to as the least rewarded risk. Traditionally operational risk was the "other risks" category with market and credit risk making up the rest of the risk universe for a firm. However, with the increased understanding of risk in financial services and the separate definition of areas like governance and liquidity risk, the definition of operational risk has become better understood as being the failures of people, processes, systems and external events.

The most useful way to define operational risk is to consider it as any risk created by the operational aspects of a firm. These are the everyday items like the operation of cash desk, computer systems backups and outside factors like power failures. This presents an interesting aspect of operational risk; it is the risk that is not rewarded.

Operational risk means the risk of loss (financial or otherwise) resulting from:

- Inadequate or failed internal processes or systems
- Any failure by persons connected with the firm
- Legal risk (including exposure to fines, penalties or damages as well as associated legal costs)
- External events

Examples of operational risks include hardware or software failures, inadequate business continuity plans, misuse of confidential information, data entry errors, and natural disasters.

Unlike operational risk, other risk types can have a reward – balanced by increased risk – when they are increased. Thus, a firm may take on more investment risk to bring an increased return – the firm may move from investing in lower yield bonds like those from large EU countries into corporate bonds. The expectation in this decision is a larger return with an acceptance of the increased risk of loss due to the different nature of the corporate bond.

However, a firm would not be wise to take on increased operational risk – no firm is going to place its computer centre in a flood plain and expect a reward. To expand the analogy, operational risk can be compared to activities such as operating a space program – there is little notice of the ongoing activities by most people, but an outcry when something goes wrong.

Types of Operational Risk

The Basel II Committee defines operational risk as:

"The risk of loss resulting from inadequate or failed internal processes, people and systems or from external events."

Related to this is the Basel II event types, outlined within Annex 7 to provide the category, definition, and examples of operational risks. Using the seven event type categories as listed by Basel II, a focused approach can be taken by firms on operational risk. Many firms struggle at first with operational risk and what is within their risk framework. The result is an operational risk register with an excess of items and inaction from too many items being managed at once.

The following lists the official Basel II defined event types with some simple examples for each category:

- Internal Fraud - misappropriation of assets, tax evasion, bribery
- External Fraud - theft of information, hacking damage, third-party theft and forgery
- Employment Practices and Workplace Safety - discrimination, workers compensation, employee health and safety
- Clients, Products, & Business Practices - market manipulation, antitrust, improper trade, product defects, fiduciary breaches
- Damage to Physical Assets - natural disasters, terrorism, vandalism
- Business Disruption and Systems Failures - utility disruptions, software failures, hardware failures

- Execution, Delivery, & Process Management - data entry errors, accounting errors, failed mandatory reporting, negligent loss of client assets

By taking related work from the Basel Committee, these categories can be linked back to specific operational areas within a firm. By using the risk subcategories listed above, a more focused approach should be found to operational risk in any firm. Thus, a conversation about operational risk could look at focusing on the "Execution, Delivery & Process Management" area with a focus on "Customer Intake and Documentation" and a review of whether the risk "Legal documents missing / incomplete" is relevant for a process such as account opening or the creation of a loan for customer.

5.3 Operational Risk Detail

Operational Risk and Internal Controls

Internal controls are a technique to allow a firm to meet objectives in operational and other forms of risk management, provide reliable management reporting, and help ensure compliance with external regulations and internal policies. Internal controls are a key element of the Sarbanes–Oxley Act of 2002, which resulted in improvements in internal control in United States public corporations, some of which had operations in Ireland. This introduced a wide audience to techniques such as the COSO Internal Control-Integrated Framework . In COSO, internal controls are defined as a process put in place by a firm's board of directors, management, and other officers, designed to provide reasonable assurance regarding the achievement of objectives relating to operations, reporting, and compliance.

COSO defines internal control as having five components:

- Control Environment: Sets the tone for the organization, influencing the control consciousness of its people with a "tone from the top".
- Risk Assessment: The identification and analysis of relevant risks to the achievement of objectives, forming a basis for how risks should be managed.
- Information and Communication: Systems or processes that enable people to carry out their responsibilities around control, reporting, and other activities.
- Control Activities: The policies and procedures that help ensure the firm carried out its objectives in a controlled manner.
- Monitoring: Ensuring the quality of internal control performance over time.

The key to the integrated framework process is controls – these can be defined into three major types:

- Preventive Controls: These are intended to prevent an incident from occurring (e.g., passwords on a system).
- Detective Controls: These are intended to identify and characterize an incident in progress (e.g., review of logons to a system).

- Corrective Controls: These are intended to limit the extent of any damage caused by the incident (e.g., backup of data on a system).

Using a payments example, each user should have a single logon to the payment system and no user should have the ability to enter and approve the same payment – this is the preventive control. A review of users and logons to the system should be the detective control to see if a user has more than one logon. Finally, a review of all payments in the payment system log against the payment instructions received on emails would allow an understanding of the incorrect payments and the actions required to correct any mis-payments.

5.4 Operational Risk Events

Understanding the causes and lessons learned from operational risk events can be a way to bring value from the management of operational risk.

What is an Operational Event?

Extending the definition from prior section, an operational risk event can be defined as "an unexpected profit or loss due to inadequate or failed internal processes, people and systems, or from external events". It is a best practice to investigate and report on losses that could have occurred but were avoided– these are known as near miss events. While unexpected profits are sometimes not included in the definition of such events, it is prudent to review such items as an unexpected operational risk related profit on something like investment activities, which could just as easily have been an unexpected loss.

While well-known operational risk events have included the collapse of Barings Bank due to the rogue trader Nick Leeson, most operational risk events are much smaller in value and occur more often. Examples of these may include:

- Losses of business due to utility or IT outages. It can be difficult to put a figure on such outages. One approach may be to take the turnover for the year for the firm and use this to work out the business lost during the outage. An allowance should be made for any business that took place despite the outage.
- Hacking damage to IT assets such as the website. Costs for such an event can include the fees to the website contractor to restore the site to its original format and content.
- Lost data and the effort to recover it. If a back-up of the IT systems is not completed correctly or the back-up data becomes corrupted there may be significant loss.

By reviewing the operations of a firm through methods such as process mapping, and reviewing the examples of operational losses from Basel II, typical operational risk events can be identified and documented.

Once an operational risk event has been identified, a template like the one shown in figure 22 can capture the information related to the event.

OPERATIONAL RISK INCIDENT REPORT

Title of Report:	
Contact:	
Department:	
Compliled by:	
Date of Incident:	
Date Detected:	
Date Reported to Risk:	
Reported to Board:	
Date Reported to Board:	
Brief Summary of Incident	
Brief Summary of the Cause	
Lessons Learned	
Summary of Actions Agreed	
Event type	
Basel Category	
Loss / Profit in Euro	
Cost Centre/ Department	

Figure 22: Sample Operational Risk Incident Report

Having an agreed template for recording operational events brings a standard approach to the identification, investigation, and reporting of risks within the firm.

Use the following guidance for completing each cell in the template:

- Title of Report: A simple title to allow quick and informal reference.
- Unique Identifier: It is best to have a unique identifier for each event.
- Contact: The name and position of the person who is the contact for this event. This contact is not the Risk Management person.
- Department: The department that the event relates to.
- Compiled by: The name of the individual who compiled the report. This may be someone different from the contact.
- Date of event: The date that the event happened. This can be different to when it was detected.
- Date Detected: The date the event was noticed. A long difference between when the event occurred and when it was noticed can be a concern.
- Date Reported to Risk: The date the event was reported to the risk department or office.
- Reported to Board: A yes/no response as to whether the event has been reported to the board (or management). A determination on which events at a certain threshold should be agreed upon for reporting to the board or management.
- Date Reported to Board: If "yes" picked in the field above, the date the event was reported to the board or management.

- Brief Summary of event: A short summary of what occurred – remember to use who, what, when, how, and why when providing the summary.
- Brief Summary of the Cause: What caused the issue, remember to consider the internal control environment as part of this review:
  - A control in place but not effective;
  - A control in place, but not followed;
  - No control in place of a known risk; or,
  - No control in place for an unknown risk.
- Lessons Learned: What has the organization learned from this event and what will be done differently in the future?
- Preventive Actions: What will be done to prevent this type of event occurring again. Details of actions can be filled out in the "Action" tab.
- Event Type: Near miss, Loss or Profit, remember a profit could just as easily have been a loss.
- Basel Category: The Basel Operational Risk Categories as listed earlier in this chapter.
- Loss / Profit in local currency: The cost to the organization.
- Cost Centre / Department: Which cost centre or department is taking the cost for this event. Documenting this cost allows reporting back to the accounting or finance system.

Reporting of operational risk events should be part of a defined process that ensures more material items are properly investigated and that lessons are learned from such events.

5.5 Summary

In this chapter you have learned the amount of work that is needed to manage operational risk in a firm.

Chapter 6: Strategic and Business Model Risk

6.1 Introduction

With the financial crisis of 2007-08, more focus was put on the overall performance of a firm. Many risk management processes now include the management of strategic and business model risk. These are topics that the risk manager should be aware of and work to manage.

Strategy and business model risk relate to the ability of a firm to create a sustainable business model and the related strategic plan. Related items, such as a shrinking loan book, may be managed at the credit risk level, but the risk manager needs to be able to see any root cause of this issue.

A related topic many be environmental risk, that is the risk to the firm from the external operating environment – these may be items like the local or national economy or financial services specific items like new regulations.

6.2 Why Strategic Risk?

The Changing Role of the Risk Manager

Many risk managers started their careers in a specific risk area such as credit or market risk. However, a lesson learned from the financial crisis was that this "silo-ed" approach was not ideal. Whether it was internal parties like risk managers or external parties like financial regulators, not looking at firm as a whole lead to financial services firms adopting strategies or business models that were not sustainable or became unsustainable within larger market issues.

An early example was Northern Rock in the United Kingdom. Northern Rock, formerly the Northern Rock Building Society, had a long history going back to the Northern Counties Permanent Building Society established in 1850 and the Rock Building Society established in 1865. In the 1990s Northern Rock chose to demutualise as a building society and float on the stock exchange as a bank.

Northern Rock then entered into an aggressive growth period by developing and implementing a business plan that borrowed heavily in the UK and international money markets, extended mortgages to customers based on this funding, and then reselling these mortgages on international capital markets.

In August 2007, global demand from investors for these securitised mortgages fell sharply and Northern Rock became unable to repay loans from the money market. By September 2007, the bank sought and received a liquidity support facility from the Bank of England, to replace funds it was unable to raise from the money market.

While the failure of Northern Rock would seem to relate to liquidity issues, at the heart of its failure was a business model that was not viable during periods of financial instability. The bank's failure brought this idea to the fore during the following larger financial crisis when parties such as financial regulators began to add environmental, strategic, and business model risk to their work.

Environmental risk - Considering the Business Environment

Environmental risk is not related to the environment in the potential threat of adverse effects on living organisms and environment by emissions or waste. Rather it is to do with the external environment a firm operates in, including the economic and regulatory environment.

Macro-economic risk factors make themselves felt through domestic and international developments. Macroeconomic item that generates such risk include unemployment rates, monetary policy changes such as interest rates, housing starts and even commodity prices such as oil and gold. Political changes in places like Eastern Europe have resulted in markets for global products and services that did not exist 25 years ago, and the rise of the internet has allowed such products to be sold from and to any location on the globe.

Sector specific considerations must be assessed as different industries and subsets of firms face a similar macro environment but different industry dynamics. Recent years have seen turmoil in the financial services markets and the demise of some well-known firms such as the investment bank Lehman Brothers, collapsing in 2008 as a result of more financial turmoil. The fall in interest rates has affected all financial services firms from insurance firms, trying to make a return on their assets to maintain their profits, to pension funds, trying to ensure a return that will allow the resources for their members to retire.

There has been encroachment on the traditional banking members from groups like mobile phone service providers that use their deep market penetration and knowledge of their customers to sell banking and insurance products that were traditionally sold by banks or brokers. Finally, an outcome of the recent crisis, both nationally and internationally has been a huge increase in financial services regulation.

To allow a firm to demonstrate that it has considered environmental risk, the firm should include environmental scanning in its strategic management. Environmental scanning is a process used to gather information about an organization's environment to inform decision-making and strategic planning. The environmental scan collects information from publicly available information and from key stakeholders, such as the board, existing service providers, like the external auditor, and other thought leaders. It is preferable for the environmental scan process to cumulate in a group workshop, preferably with an external facilitator.

The information from the environmental scan informs the strategic planning process but should not act as the sole driver of the strategic plan. Environmental scans provide important inputs from different stakeholders into shaping the future directions of the organization, including from people who are not engaged in the strategic planning. With the information from a systematic environmental scan in hand, an organization can develop and refine a strategic plan with awareness of its organizational context. This information helps an organization determine strategic goals and strategies that are relevant and effective.

A useful environmental scanning tool is the PESTEL analysis, displayed in figure 23. PESTEL groups the factors which organizations must be aware of and analyze as external influences affecting a business.

The six groups of factors within PESTEL are:

- Political: the current and potential influences from political pressures
- Economic: the impact of local, national and world economy
- Social: the ways in which changes in society affect the organization
- Technological: the effect of new and emerging technology
- Environmental: local, national and world environmental issues
- Legal: the effect of legislation in locally and other countries

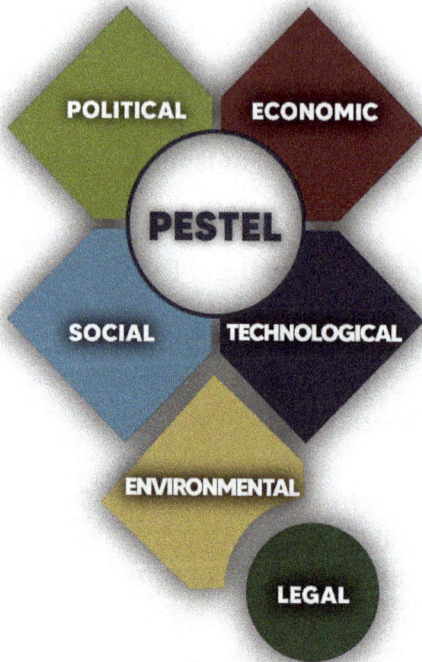

Figure 23: PESTEL

By starting with a PESTEL analysis, a firm shows it has considered its environmental risk before it moves on to the rest of the strategic planning process. A possible set of environmental risks to consider, based on the PESTEL approach, could be:

- Political: any political response to the 2000s financial crisis may have good or bad consequences for financial services firms.
- Economic: local economic issues may affect some financial services firms. Some regions were badly hit

by the Great Recession and did not recover as quickly as others.

- Social: some financial services firms find their customers are of an older generation. There are opportunities in marketing to this age group. Conversely there is an opportunity to try and market to a younger generation who may not have thought of using the firm before.
- Technological: the rise of the internet has been mirrored by an increase in online banking. Financial services firms may need to expand their online offering to attract and retain some members. However, there are some customers who prefer a local branch that they can call into to do their business.
- Environmental: flooding has been an issue for some people's home in the 21st century – this may affect insurance sales and products.
- Legal: an effect of the financial crisis has been a huge increase in the demands of governance, risk management and compliance for financial services firms.

6.3 Strategic Risk Tools

With the external environment considered, the risk manager can move on to consider relevant internal risks for the firm.

Strategy is a high-level plan for an organization to achieve one or more goals under conditions of uncertainty with limited resources. Strategy involves two key elements, formulation of the strategy and implementation of the strategy. The unsuccessful achievement of either of these is at the heart of strategic risk. Formulation of the strategy involves the already covered analysis of the environment the organization is operating in. The firm must then make some decisions on the goals by developing the strategic plan.

SWOT Analysis

A SWOT analysis allows for a more focused review of the possibilities for the firm. A SWOT analysis identifies the Strengths, Weaknesses, Opportunities and Threats for an organization. SWOT is a basic but powerful model that assesses what an organization can and cannot do as well as its potential opportunities and threats.

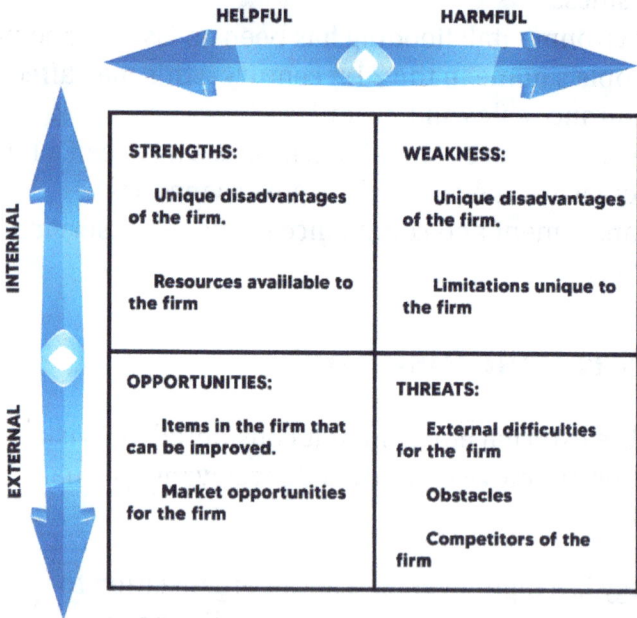

	HELPFUL	HARMFUL
INTERNAL	**STRENGTHS:** Unique disadvantages of the firm. Resources availlable to the firm	**WEAKNESS:** Unique disadvantages of the firm. Limitations unique to the firm
EXTERNAL	**OPPORTUNITIES:** Items in the firm that can be improved. Market opportunities for the firm	**THREATS:** External difficulties for the firm Obstacles Competitors of the firm

Figure 24: SWOT

To perform a SWOT analysis, a group of staff and an external facilitator should take the information from the previous environmental analysis (PESTEL) and separate it into internal (strengths and weaknesses) and external issues (Opportunities and Threats), as shown in figure 24. Once this task is completed, the SWOT analysis process helps to determine what may assist the firm in accomplishing its objectives, and what obstacles must be overcome or minimized to achieve the desired results.

When using a SWOT analysis, it is important to remain realistic about the strengths and weaknesses of the firm. Participants should distinguish between where the firm is at currently, where it could be in 1 year, and then in 3 to 5 years.

A SWOT analysis provides a clearer understanding of:

- Strengths: characteristics of the firm that give it an advantage over others (e.g., it may have large cash reserves to invest in new projects).
- Weaknesses: characteristics that place the firm at a disadvantage relative to others (e.g., there may be an inexperienced management team).
- Opportunities: elements that the firm could exploit to its advantage (e.g., a new market that the firm may enter).
- Threats: elements in the business environment that could cause trouble for the firm (existing or new competitors).

The SWOT analysis should be kept short and simple - complexity may result in over-analysis. Once completed, the results should be documented and used as part of the input for the next step of the process – developing the business model.

6.4 Business Model Risk

Once the elements of a strategy have been identified, the elements can be assembled into a business model. A business model describes how an organization creates value for its customers by developing a Customer Value Proposition. The customer value proposition is a statement that encapsulates why a consumer should buy a product or use a service from the firm.

The firm should use the output of its PESTEL and SWOT analysis to assemble an offering for a potential customer. The offering should be sufficient to convince that customer that the offered product or service will add more value or better solve a problem than other similar offerings from competitors.

Business Model Canvas

The Business Model Canvas is a visual method used to assemble a business model. The Canvas was initially proposed by Alexander Osterwalder and was based on his earlier work on a Business Model Ontology. It has gained a strong acceptance as a strategic management template for developing new or documenting existing business models. The canvas provides an excellent way to capture, discuss, and agree on a business model.

Figure 25 provides a visual of a Business Model Canvas with elements describing a firm's value proposition, infrastructure, members, and finances. Using it usually works best in groups of four to eight people. Figure 25 may be printed out on a large surface or projected onto a surface. The group can then use sticky notes or whiteboard markers to place items identified from the PESTEL and SWOT analysis into the boxes in the business model canvas. As sticky notes are used the group do not have to write permanently on the canvas – changes can be made throughout the activity and the final content can be captured and documented.

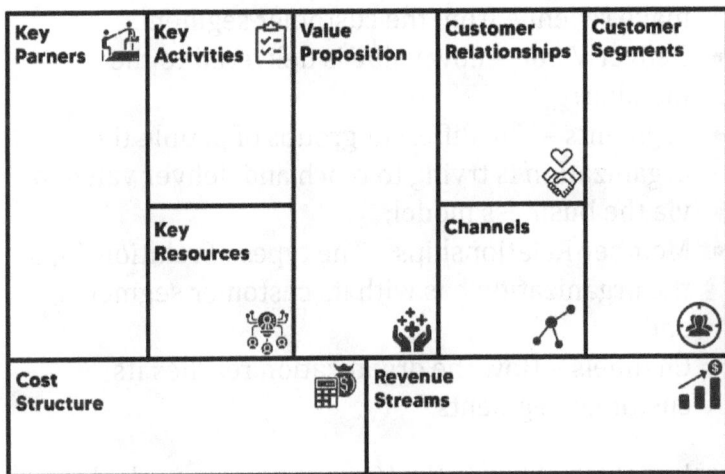

Figure 25: A business model canvas

The canvas is broken up into nine sections that belong to four areas:

- Create Value - how the business model will create value for members:

- Key Activities – What will the organization to make the business model work;
- Key Partners – The suppliers and partners that help the organization make the business model work; and,
- Key Resources – The most important assets the organization use to create value;
- Capture Value – the costs and revenues related to the business model:
- Cost Structure – The organization costs involved in running the business and delivering on the business model; and,
- Revenue Streams – Where the organization will make revenue from the customer segments
- Deliver Value – how value is delivered to the member:
- Segments – The different groups of people the organization is trying to reach and deliver value to via the business model;
- Member Relationships – The types of relationships the organization has with its customer segments; and,
- Channels – How the organization reaches its customer segments.

At the center of this is the Value Proposition, the key ideas that create value for the customer segments.

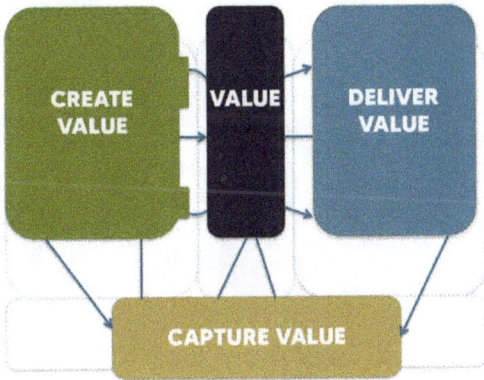

Figure 26: Value Proposition

The risk manager should be part of this process as it is here that critical elements of the business model can be identified and any threats to them discussed and documented. In addition, by carrying out such an inclusive process, the final business model should be one that is more likely to succeed when the firm moves to implementation.

6.5 Summary

The risk manager can bring a great deal to a firm in their management of strategic risk by advising of threats and opportunities and helping to bring this into the strategic and business planning process.

Afterword

You should now be able to explain what risk is and how it is not always a bad thing. Being able to understand and use risk management will benefit you greatly in your life and career. You may decide to go on and understand more about some of the elements that were introduced in this book, such as the risk register and risk appetite.

In the other risk categories, you can reflect on topics such as:

- Market risk and how stress testing may be used to understand the risks for a certain financial firm
- Credit risk and the credit product lifecycle
- Liquidity risk and how it is part of asset liability management, and how to manage this risk
- Operational risk and how lessons learned can come from investigating operational risk events
- Strategic and business model risk and how this is something that the 21st century risk manager should be aware of and able to manage

Finally you can reflect on how risk management may be applied in your own organization, be it in financial services or elsewhere.

Learn more

Explore more of the PRMIA learning and certification programs such as:

- Professional Risk Manager (PRM™) Designation: Endorsed by leading businesses and universities, the PRM is the global standard for the world's top financial risk professionals - essential to practicing industry Chief Risk Officers.
- Professional Operational Risk Manager (ORM™) Designation: Developed to recognize the competencies of operational risk leaders, the Professional ORM Designation program is for professionals leading their organizations through operational risks globally.
- Associate PRM Certificate: The Associate PRM Certificate is designed for staff entering the risk management profession, or other users such as auditing, accounting, legal, and systems development personnel who need to understand fundamental risk management methods and practices.
- Operational Risk Management Certificate: The Operational Risk Management Certificate is designed to deliver a deep, practical understanding of operational risk management frameworks and measurement methodologies in financial institutions.

PRMIA certifications and certificates are recognized by leading global institutes.

About the Author

Justin McCarthy has worked in roles in many firms, including Bank of America, Merrill Lynch, PricewaterhouseCoopers, and with the Irish Financial Regulator. This work has allowed him to see the changes in risk management through and beyond the global financial crisis of 2007-08. His work on the PRISM risk-based supervision framework with the Irish Regulator included exposure to banking, funds, and insurance risk practices as well as the quantitative work related to impact models and the challenge in feeding valid financial data to these models.

Justin is Chair of the Global Board of the Professional Risk Managers' International Association Institute (PRMIA Institute), the research arm of the professional body and education organization for risk managers. PRMIA is a global association with a network of over 50,000 risk professionals around the world.

Justin currently works as a Strategy, Governance, Risk and Compliance Consultant and also lectures and provides learning opportunities. He works with several FinTech companies and start-ups in this capacity.

Justin has a BSc from University College Cork and an MBA from the Michael Smurfit Graduate School of Business at University College Dublin and is studying for his Corporate Director Certificate at Harvard Business School.

He is originally from Schull, West Cork and lives in Cork City, Ireland.

About PRMIA

The Professional Risk Managers' International Association (PRMIA) is a non-profit professional association, governed by a Board of Directors directly elected by its global membership. PRMIA is represented globally by 46 chapters in major cities around the world, led by Regional Directors appointed by the Board.

Mission and Objectives

Established in 2002 by a volunteer group of risk industry professionals, our mission is to provide an open forum for the development and promotion of the risk profession. To accomplish this mission, the objectives are:

- To be a leader of industry opinion and a proponent for the risk management profession Drive the integration of practice and theory and certify the credentials of professional risk managers
- Connect practitioners, researchers, students and others interested in the field of risk management

- Be global in focus, promoting cross-cultural ethical standards, serving emerging as well as more developed markets
- Work with other professional associations in furtherance of our mission

Community and Membership

We provide an open forum for the development and promotion of the risk profession. PRMIA is a non-profit, member-led association dedicated to defining and implementing the best practices of risk management through education; webinar, online, classroom and in-house training; events; networking; and online resources.

Learn more at www.prmia.org/Membership.

Professional Designations

Professional Risk Manager (PRM™) Designation

Endorsed by leading businesses and universities, the PRM is the global standard for the world's top financial risk professionals-essential to practicing industry CROs.

Learn more at www.prmia.org/PRM.

Professional Operational Risk Manager (ORM) Designation

Developed by a broad coalition of industry leaders to recognize the competencies of the leading operational risk leaders around the world.

Learn more at www.prmia.org/ORM.

Certificates in Risk Management

PRM™ Certificate Programs for Students

Students currently enrolled in a degree program are eligible to take the PRM examinations as part of a special certificate program. By passing the PRM examinations, you have evidence that you understand the fundamentals important to sound financial risk management practices.

Learn more at www.prmia.org/Student.

Associate PRM Certificate

The Associate PRM Certificate is designed for staff entering the risk management profession, or other users such as auditing, accounting, legal, and systems development personnel who need to understand fundamental risk management methods and practices.

Operational Risk Management Certificate

The Operational Risk Management (ORM) Certificate covers the practical understanding of operational risk management frameworks and measurement methodologies in financial institutions.

Credit and Counterparty Risk Management Certificate

The Credit and Counterparty Management (CCRM) Certificate covers a deep and practical understanding of credit risk analysis frameworks.

Market, Liquidity and Asset Liability Risk Management Certificate

The Market, Liquidity and Asset Liability Risk Management (MLARM) Certificate covers the underlying principles of market risk and asset liability management.

Certificates of Practice

Certificate of Team Leadership in Advanced Operational Risk

The Certificate of Team Leadership in Advanced Operational Risk provides operational risk leaders and teams with proven solutions for solving current and emerging operational risk issues for their organizations. The program is intended for those leading the efforts to institute or maintain operational risk management frameworks within their institutions.

Certificate of Advanced Leadership in Crisis Risk Management

The Certificate in Advanced Leadership in Crisis Risk Management provides risk leaders the skills and tools to lead efforts to prepare for crises within their institutions and implement preventions that will reduce the likelihood and impact of any crisis and enable disaster recovery when necessary.

Risk Resources

Our publications provide you with access to some of the highest quality and most relevant writing for professional risk managers. Members have access to a wealth of online resources including a Jobs Board with risk management job openings in cities around the world, links to past presentations and papers, and much more.

Learning Programs

PRMIA CRL
CONTINUED RISK LEARNING

Authentic. Accessible. Relevant.

Learning and thought leadership to advance your career

We offer professional development for risk professionals at any stage in their career, from entry courses to help individuals gain entry into a risk related role, to advanced topics in financial risk management that offer practitioners opportunities to enhance their skills.

Learn more at www.prmia.org/learning.

Global Presence

We are active in nearly every major financial center worldwide and provides an extensive and engaged network of risk professionals.

We offers 200 meetings each year through local chapters, giving members access to the best practices of the global risk profession and to a local network of colleagues. Executive staff and board members can take advantage of the Risk Leader Program, which connects a global network of Chief Risk Officers and the most senior risk professionals.

Professional Risk Managers' International Association
(PRMIA)

9.951 42335CB00014B/1638 [2084318847]

www.ingramcontent.com/pod-product-compliance
Lightning Source LLC
Chambersburg PA
CBHW060249030426
42335CB00014B/1638